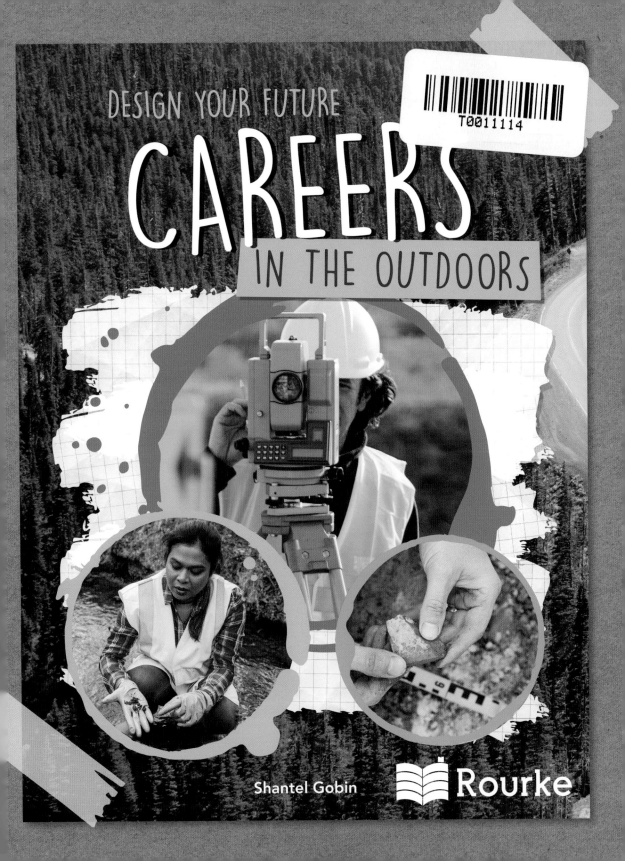

DESIGN YOUR FUTURE

CAREERS
IN THE OUTDOORS

Shantel Gobin

Rourke

Before Reading: *Building Background Knowledge and Vocabulary*

Building background knowledge can help children process new information and build upon what they already know. Before reading a book, it is important to tap into what children already know about the topic. This will help them develop their vocabulary and increase their reading comprehension.

Questions and Activities to Build Background Knowledge:

1. Look at the front cover of the book and read the title. What do you think this book will be about?
2. What do you already know about this topic?
3. Take a book walk and skim the pages. Look at the table of contents, photographs, captions, and bold words. Did these text features give you any information or predictions about what you will read in this book?

Vocabulary: *Vocabulary Is Key to Reading Comprehension*

Use the following directions to prompt a conversation about each word.

- Read the vocabulary words.
- What comes to mind when you see each word?
- What do you think each word means?

Vocabulary Words:

- certifications
- internship
- qualifications
- skills
- specialty
- worksite

During Reading: *Reading for Meaning and Understanding*

To achieve deep comprehension of a book, children are encouraged to use close reading strategies. During reading, it is important to have children stop and make connections. These connections result in deeper analysis and understanding of a book.

Close Reading a Text

During reading, have children stop and talk about the following:

- Any confusing parts
- Any unknown words
- Text to text, text to self, text to world connections
- The main idea in each chapter or heading

Encourage children to use context clues to determine the meaning of any unknown words. These strategies will help children learn to analyze the text more thoroughly as they read.

When you are finished reading this book, turn to the next-to-last page for **After-Reading Questions** and an **Activity**.

TABLE OF CONTENTS

OUTSIDE THE OFFICE

Your interests can start you on the path to a job you will love. Have you ever thought an office job wasn't for you? Do you enjoy the outdoors? Are you a nature lover? A career in the outdoors may be just right! Let's explore different career paths that all lead to a life outside the office.

Keep an eye out for these icons to learn more about how to achieve your goals:

Minimum education/training required

Average time commitment (beyond a high school degree or GED)

Ways to boost your **qualifications**

qualifications (kwahl-uh-fi-KAY-shuhnz): skills or abilities that make you able to do a job

GROUNDSKEEPER

The clue is in the name. Groundskeepers keep grounds! They maintain the health and appearance of any outdoor space. This can be a small backyard, a community garden, or even a stadium. The job varies depending on the location. It can include mowing lawns, trimming hedges, or shoveling snow. Groundskeepers do what it takes to keep their **worksite** in tip-top shape. They also purchase, store, and maintain the equipment needed for their outdoor spaces.

worksite (WURK-site): an area where people work

certifications (sur-tuh-fuh-KAY-shuhnz): documents that state that special qualifications within a field have been met

GED or high school diploma
Experience

No set time

Work for a landscaping company
Certifications in landscaping or horticulture

LANDSCAPE ARCHITECT

Who put the swings next to the slide? A landscape architect, that's who. Landscape architects design outdoor locations. Their worksite can range from a city park to a forest trail. These professionals spend a lot of time on site to come up with ideas for the space. Some time has to be spent at a desk to draw up the plans. Hopefully, the desk is outside too! If not, landscape architects make it back outdoors to work with contractors and other professionals to bring their ideas to life.

Bachelor's degree in landscape architecture
Pass a licensing exam

4 years

Internship

internship (IN-turn-ship): a job in which someone who is learning a skill or job works with an expert in the field

WELDER

Welders are into heavy metal. Not the music...the material. Welders use heat to join different types of metal together. Many spend their time outdoors as sheet metal, construction, or even underwater welders! Underwater welders are some of the highest paid in their field. That is because it can be dangerous and they need to be highly skilled. They work directly in water or in a special chamber that is lowered into the water. Underwater welders work on repairing things like pipelines, ships, and dams.

GED or high school diploma

No set time

Certification in welding
Associate's degree

Hacks & Hints

Some high schools offer welding courses that are a great way to get a head start on a career in welding. Getting an associate's degree in welding technology will give you a competitive advantage and allow you to achieve higher level positions.

Construction welders are one of the most common types of welders. They can work on the ground joining gas lines, or they can be high above the ground building skyscrapers. The **skills** needed depend on the worksite. Commercial sites may require knowledge of advanced plumbing or ventilation systems. More complex jobs will require a higher level of training.

skills (skilz): the ability to do something well, usually as a result of training or practice

OUTDOOR ADVENTURE GUIDE

Lead the way! Outdoor adventure guides take people on anything from afternoon hikes to month-long treks through nature. These guides work anywhere people want to hike! Guides spend a lot of time exploring the environment in which they work. They educate their groups about the area and get everyone through the trip safely. Since they spend most of their time outdoors, weather conditions impact the work schedule.

🎓 Experience in your area of interest (hiking, backpacking, cycling, camping)

🕐 No set time

⊕ Wilderness First Responder (WFR) certification Customer service experience

Hacks & Hints

Most outdoor adventure guide positions prefer someone with a WFR certification. To really give yourself a leg up, get additional certifications in your area of interest. Want to lead the way through mountains? Get certified through the American Mountain Guides Association (AMGA). Is water more your speed? Look into certifications from the American Canoe Association (ACA).

AG PILOT

   Is flying in your future? Ag pilots, short for agricultural pilots, fly small planes to spray fields. They fly at low heights to deliver chemicals to protect or produce crops. This includes fertilizers, fungicides, and pesticides. Ag pilots can work from rural airports. If they own their own crop-dusting plane, they can work for themselves and have individual farm owners or corporate farms as their clients.

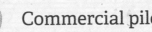

- Commercial pilot license

- 250 hours

- Bachelor's degree in related field

SURVEYOR

Do you love math? Well, that doesn't mean you have to be stuck at a desk! Surveyors collect measurements of different outdoor locations. There are many types of surveyors. Some establish official boundaries of land, water, and air for local agencies. Others may choose a **specialty** that is related to their interests. For example, those interested in criminal justice could become forensic surveyors and provide landscape evidence for court cases.

specialty (SPESH-uhl-tee): the skill or area of study that you are particularly good at

Bachelor's degree
Pass a licensing exam

4 years

Experience with computer–aided
design software

Travel is often part of any surveyor's job. This can mean traveling around town or traveling to measure the length of a newly discovered island! A job like that may be too big for one person. That's when a crew of surveyors would be needed to tackle the task. The most experienced will likely be the team leader and direct day-to-day work activities for the whole team. The leader also makes more money!

WILDLAND FIREFIGHTER

If you're up for an adrenaline-filled career, wildland firefighting will offer plenty of it! Wildland firefighters fight wildfires. They may fly in helicopters or hike mountains to get to the fire. Specialty crews, such as smokejumpers and hotshots, require extra training and experience. Smokejumpers parachute from planes to put out fires in locations hard to reach on foot. Hotshot crews go where equipment can't reach the hottest part of a wildfire. They use shovels and chain saws to clear away brush that could catch fire and cut down trees to suppress fire.

- GED or high school diploma
  Training program

- 3,000 hours

- Join a volunteer fire department
  Associate's or bachelor's degree in fire science

RAFTING GUIDE

Row, row, row, your boat not so gently down the stream. Rafting guides lead whitewater rafting trips. They also prepare the rafts, teach guests about safety procedures, and give crash courses in rafting. Some rafting trips can be overnight. That means rafting guides also need wilderness survival skills.

River experience

No set time

Certifications in first aid and CPR
Associate's degree in outdoor education
or recreation

Hints & Hacks

A lot of places that employ rafting guides will offer training and certifications in rafting after you start. Getting certifications in first aid and rescue will give you a leg up.

GEOLOGIST

Rock the world with this career. Geologists spend their time outdoors exploring Earth's surfaces. They examine natural materials such as rocks, metals, or oils. Geologists also study natural disasters or events. This may include collecting samples at the site of earthquakes, landslides, and floods. Some geologists also work to figure out how to extract resources from nature. They may spend some of their time in labs, examining samples from their sites.

Bachelor's degree

4 years

Master's degree or PhD

There are many specialties in this career, usually connected to the geologist's interests. Someone who likes volcanoes may become a volcanologist. They monitor eruptions and collect samples of hot lava. If someone is interested in the ocean, they may become a marine geologist. They learn about how events that occur at the ocean floor affect the rest of the environment.

MEMORY GAME

Look at the pictures. What do you remember reading on the pages where each image appeared?

INDEX

AFTER—READING QUESTIONS

1. Which job can get you close to a volcano?

2. What do welders do?

3. Who needs a pilot's license to work?

4. Name a specialty crew of wildland firefighters and what they do.

5. Who would you call if you were planning a backpacking trip?

ACTIVITY

Make a list of your interests and all the things you like to do for fun. Which career in the outdoors has the most in common with your list? Look up careers that are similar to your chosen career in the outdoors. Make a list of the ones that catch your eye. Find out more about these careers, such as the schooling or training you need and how long it will take you to reach your goal.

ABOUT THE AUTHOR

Shantel Gobin loves helping people grow and achieve their goals. She enjoys writing to inspire new ways of thinking. It is her goal to create a generation of lifelong learners. She lives in Brooklyn, New York, where she works as a school psychologist and author.

www.rourkebooks.com

PHOTO CREDITS: cover, title page: ©Carmen Martínez Torrón/ Getty Images, ©anandaBGD/ Getty Images, ©SolStock/ Getty Images, ©BartCo/ Getty Images; cover, title page, pages 8-9, 12, 15, 18-19, 29: ©marekuliasz/ Shutterstock.com; back cover: ©Olya Fedorova/ Shutterstock.com, ©gdvcom/ Shutterstock.com; title page, TOC, pages 3-32: ©nortongo/ Getty Images; title page, 4-8, 10-12, 14-30: ©Flas100/ Shutterstock.com; TOC, pages 4, 6, 14, 22, 30-32: ©My Life Graphic/ Shutterstock.com; pages 4-5: ©V. Smirnov/ Shutterstock.com; pages 4, 7, 8, 10, 14, 17, 19, 22-24, 26: ©13ree.design/ Shutterstock.com; pages 4, 7, 8, 10, 14, 17, 19, 22-24, 26: ©RaiDztor/ Shutterstock.com; pages 4, 7, 8, 10, 12-17, 19, 23, 24, 26: ©MichaelJayBerlin/ Shutterstock.com; pages 7, 23: ©Realstockvector/ Shutterstock.com; page 7: ©Kent E Roberts/ Shutterstock.com; pages 7, 30: ©Alexandros Michailidis/ Shutterstock.com; pages 8-9: ©CHUNYIP WONG/ Getty Images; pages 8-9: ©Toa55/ Getty Images; page 9: ©sturti/ Getty Images; page 11: U.S. Navy/Mass Communication Specialist Senior Chief Andrew McKaskle/ Wikimedia Commons; pages 11, 30: ©Sergei Butorin/ Shutterstock.com; page 12: ©zhengzaishuru/ Shutterstock.com; page 13: ©ME Image/ Shutterstock.com; pages 15, 30: ©PamelaJoeMcFarlane; pages 14-15: ©FG Trade/ Getty Images; page 16: ©Lightguard/ Getty Images; pages 16-17: ©SteveMcsweeny/ Getty Images; page 18: ©CatEyePerspective/ Getty Images; pages 18-19, 30: ©Vane Nunes/ Shutterstock.com; page 19: ©New Africa/ Shutterstock.com; pages 20-21: ©stock_colors/ Getty Images; pages 20-21: ©SolStock/ Getty Images; page 21: ©CasarsaGuru/ Getty Images; pages 22-23: ©Toa55/ Shutterstock.com; pages 23, 30: ©Sobrevolando Patagonia/ Shutterstock.com; page 24: ©Ekaterina Soldatenko/ Shutterstock.com; pages 24-35: ©Phuketian.S/ Shutterstock.com; pages 27, 30: ©simonkr/ Getty Images; page 28: ©Maksym Kaharlyk/ Shutterstock.com; pages 28-29: ©jacquesvandinteren/ Getty Images; page 29: ©zaferkizilkaya/ Shutterstock.com; page 29: ©Balefire/ Shutterstock.com

Edited by: Hailey Scragg
Cover and interior design by: Alison Tracey

Library of Congress PCN Data

Careers in the Outdoors / Shantel Gobin
(Design Your Future)
   ISBN 978-1-73165-285-0 (hard cover)
   ISBN 978-1-73165-255-3 (soft cover)
   ISBN 978-1-73165-315-4 (e-book)
   ISBN 978-1-73165-345-1 (e-pub)
Library of Congress Control Number: 2021952191

Rourke Educational Media
Printed in the United States of America
01-2412211937